OTHER BOOKS OF THE WRITER

THE GOSPLE OF BANABAS
Muslims believe the Bible in use today is not the original version of the Hebrew Scriptures. They look for avenues to prove their claim even though there is none to hold on to. However, they found the so-called 'Gospel of Barnabas' which most of the early Christians did not sight. Thus, this has become their claim to prove that the ultimate life story of our Lord Jesus Christ is picturesquely told in this book and so question the authenticity of the Bible.

THE COMFORTER
John was the only apostle and evangelist who reported the last dialogue between Christ and the apostles. This happened at the Last Supper moments before Jesus' arrest. Four chapters of John's Gospel (14 to 17) are devoted to this narration and they are set out with all the grandeur and solemnity that characterize the farewell scene between the Master and His disciples. This farewell scene, containing Jesus' spiritual testament, is entirely absent from Matthew, Mark and Luke. I summarize as follows: Muslims asserted that the Paracletus Jesus Christ spoke of was Muhammad whose name they fancy to say is the translation of the word *Paracletus*.

WORSHIP ALLAH OR JAHOVAH
There are many today, including professing Christians and Muslims, who believe that Allah is the same as Jehovah. Even the Roman Catholic Church says Muslims worship the same God as Christians: "The plan of salvation also includes those who acknowledge the Creator, in the first place amongst whom are the Muslims; these profess to hold the faith of Abraham, and together with us they adore the one, merciful God, mankind's Judge on the last day". (Austin Flannery, O.P., general Editor, Vatican Council II, The Conciliar and Postconciliar Documents Costello).

MOSES AND MOHAMMED
There were hardly any two prophets who were so much alike as Moses and Muhammad. Both were given a comprehensive law and code of life. Both encountered their enemies and were victorious in miraculous ways; both were accepted as prophets and statesmen and both migrated, following conspiracies to assassinate them. Analogies between Moses and Jesus overlook not only the above similarities but other crucial ones as well. These include the natural birth, the family life and death of Moses and Muhammad but not of Jesus. Moreover Jesus' followers regarded him as the Son of God and not exclusively as a prophet of God, as Moses and Muhammad were and as Muslims believe Jesus was. So, this prophecy refers to the Prophet Muhammad and not to Jesus, because Muhammad is more like Moses than Jesus.

ISLAMIC SETS
Most people think that Islam has no divisions, because they see all of them apparently behaving in the same way or manner. Most Christians have therefore not found it necessary to investigate if there are divisions among the Muslims or not. Since there is power in knowledge, let us seek the knowledge in this matter. The reason for this study is that, I was once talking to a Muslim friend and he asked "Why do you have so many divisions in Christianity? You see I can enter in to any mosque to pray, but you can't just enter in to every church room. So you see that there is more unity in our religion than yours. So just try and submit to Allah.

The Promise, Isaac or Ishmael?

How to present
The Gospel
to a
Muslim

The Soul Winners Hand Book
Volume One

ADJEI ISHMAEL OKANG

authorHOUSE®

AuthorHouse™
1663 Liberty Drive
Bloomington, IN 47403
www.authorhouse.com
Phone: 1 (800) 839-8640

Published by AuthorHouse 06/13/2019

ISBN: 978-1-7283-1506-5 (sc)
ISBN: 978-1-7283-1505-8 (e)

Print information available on the last page.

This book is printed on acid-free paper.

Scripture taken from The Holy Bible, King James Version. Public Domain

Scripture quotations marked NIV are taken from the Holy Bible, New International Version®. NIV®. Copyright © 1973, 1978, 1984 by International Bible Society. Used by permission of Zondervan. All rights reserved. [Biblica]

Scripture quotations marked RSV are taken from the Revised Standard Version of the Bible, copyright © 1946, 1952, 1971 by the Division of Christian Education of the National Council of the Churches of Christ in the USA. Used by permission.

Dedications

This book is dedicated to those who love the Lord. To my wife Naa Patricia Okang; my daughters Angela, Adoley, Happy and Adokor and my son Nii Shidaa, may the light of the Lord shine on you. Rev. Dr. E. Markwei of Living Streams International(Ghana), my mentor and spiritual father; I salute you. Prophet Richard Owusu of Gethsemane Ministries Incorporated(USA), you made my dream come through. I could not leave out Rev. John Esubonteng and Pastor Raymond of Living Streams International, for their inspiration. I am grateful to my beloved parents, Madam Rebecca Okang and Warrant Officer I Adjetey Mc-Gershon. Miss Judith Akua Antwi of blessed memories and Linda Sarpong of N.M.I.M.R, your encouragement and help have not been in vain. And lastly, to Mr. Moses Ahun and Nana Nyarko Boateng for their encouragement and editorial services.

Acknowledgements

I have had the good fortune of reading widely from many scholars for this volume I acknowledge referencing from the materials and authors:

Kitabun Nikah (Mishkat), Mishkat Kitabul Hudud, Mishkatul Masabih, Ibn Khaldu, Mahmud. Y. Zaid, Mish Kdt, Mishkat, Helmut Gatje, Mirza Muhsin,

Preface

It is difficult for the Christian to talk about the Quran with much confidence. Often, Christians are afraid of what may be interpreted from what they say or do not know what to say at all. In several instances where some Christians have seen me with the Quran, they have said to me, "You are wasting your time." Yet, Muslims preach with the Bible because they refer to it on many occasions. The problem has to do with the amount of knowledge the Christian has concerning the Quran. The time has come for true Christians to take up the challenge to study, understand and share ideas in the Quran.

From 1984 to the mid-nineties, a group of young Christians I and started ministry work with Mr. Rocky Bell Adaturah. He taught us how to preach Christ to Muslims. I learnt a lot at his feet and I respect him highly. He is a good and selfless man. Time passed and it seemed I had forgotten everything I put down about this kind of service.

Then on 20th January, 2005, I had a dream. In the dream I was in a big room, like a conference hall. I was there with a Muslim and other people but I could not make them out. Suddenly, there was a strange sound outside and when the Muslim and I came out to check source of the sound, we saw the sky had changed; it looked like water in a swimming pool. We were still looking, when suddenly, the image of Christ appeared on the wavy sky.

"I want to show you something", the image said. He then showed us a big, nice, and clean city. In fact the city was magnificent - a place where everyone would desire to live. After some time, the city faded out.

Another city, similar to the first, was shown to us but it was on fire. He then said to us, "You have heard and read about heaven and hell. The fire you see in the city is more than what happened in Sodom and Gomorrah". When the second image faded out, He said, "I want you to know that heaven and hell are real". And then the voice said nothing more so we came back into the room.

The people were still in the room when we returned and though I still could not make them out, I asked them, "Did you also see what we saw outside?" They said they were waiting for me to come back and explain to them. I was about to start the explanation when I woke up from the dream.

I have asked myself a lot of questions since then. "Why were they relying on me, and not the Muslim, for the explanation? That was what prompted me to revisit my notes on the work I had done trying to convert Muslims to Christianity. I feel it is important for my fellow Christians to know that Muslims also need Christ.

Introduction

Many Christians forget the fact that Muslims need Christ too. One could say, "But we are all serving the same God" Have you taken it upon yourself to find out if that were true? How much knowledge do you have about Islam? Have you ever read or held the Quran?

In this study it will interest you to know that we are not serving the same God as you may have thought or heard some people claim. The Allah of the Muslims is definitely not the same as the Jehovah of the Jews and the Christians.

Islam is a religion, but Christianity is a Relationship between the Father and His children. Religions deal with 'conduct' but Christianity (Relationship) deals with 'character'. Religions say 'conduct before character'. Religion is a way through which man tries to reach God but Christianity is the way through which God reaches out to man. Christianity differs from all the religions of the world in this respect. Christianity is not a set of creeds, nor a set of doctrines, nor a body of ethics. All the other creeds and laws have been developed out of Christianity. Doctrines have been made out of its teachings, and the world's best ethics have been its product.

Christianity is not a science any more than your family is a science, but it is based on scientific fact. Christianity is not a philosophy, but it is the revelation of divine-human relationship. Christianity is not a theology; it is the reality of man's redemption and union with God Jehovah.

NOTE: *All Qur'anic readings are from The Marmaduke Pickthall Version and all Bible readings are from The King James Version unless otherwise stated.*

This book was compiled and written by:
Pastor Adjei Ishmael Okang
Gethsemane Ministry Incorporated
2 South Chester Pike, Glenolden, Pa 19036.
Email: fromisaactoishmael5@gmail.com

Chapter One

HOW TO PRESENT THE GOSPEL TO A MUSLIM

───────────────── ❋ ─────────────────

Presenting the Gospel to a Muslim can be a challenge to some Christians because they are not ready to speak to others who are not of like mind about Christ. We have been commanded to go and make all men His disciples and this we must do.

When presenting Christ to the Muslim, there are a few things that one must know and stick to:

Do not let the Muslim know that you know so much. If ego comes in, it would appear you are showing off.

Do not try to argue with them but give them space to flow. Let them feel at ease and listen.

Make sure you stick to the topic being discussed. It makes you stay focused. Going contrary to this will cause you much trouble.

Be a good listener.

Do not let them take you off your aim by compromise.

Do not be shy to admit it if you do not know the answers to questions they might ask you. Make no mistake of committing yourself to things you are not sure of. There is no shame in admitting your lack of knowledge on a particular issue but there is shame in saying things to discredit yourself. Let him or her have trust and respect for you.

Be very friendly. We are always ready to attack people that we consider as enemies. You would do well if you see him or her as a friend.

Do not raise a topic you have no idea about. Be careful not to enter into a mood of excitement. Most often you cannot think straight when you are too excited.

Do not be overtaken when he starts talking like a child. When or if you have no knowledge about something, you may ask a funny question to appear childish to someone knowledgeable in that area.

Do not ever make any attempt to condemn or judge him as he talks. When you condemn a man, you cannot win him to your side. Speak with a heart of love because you were also saved through love. Let him feel good and important.

Do not ever condemn or accept his Quran. The Quran is his final authority so be careful not to say any bad thing about it and do not accept it as an authority either.

Chapter Two

IS THE BIBLE THE WORD OF GOD?

The testimony of the Quran about the Bible - It is evident that the Quran bears witness to the fact that in Muhammad's time, there existed in Arabia both Christians and Jews, who differed from one another.

Sura 3: The Imrans (Imran): 67

Abraham (Ibrahim) was neither Jews nor Christian. He was an upright man, one who surrendered Himself to Allah. He was not a Polytheist. (Mahmud Y. Zayid)

Sura 3: The Imrans (Imran): 110

Ye are the best community that hath been raised up for mankind. Ye enjoin right conduct and forbid indecency; and ye believe in Allah. And if the people of the scripture had believed it had been better for them. Some of them are believers; but most of them are evil-livers. (M. Pickthall)

The Quran testifies to the fact that the Book from which these two religious communities received their Title still existed among them. The Quran calls it "the Book" which is made up of:

- The TAURAT => The Law – The Books of Moses.
- The ZABUR => The Psalms – The Books of David.
- The INJIL => The GOSPEL – The Books of Jesus.

THE TAURAT – THE LAW

Sura 5: The Table (Al - Maider): 44a

Lo! We did reveal the Torah. Where is guidance and light, by which the prophets who surrendered (onto Allah) judge the Jews and the rabbis and the priests (judged) by such of Allah's scripture as they were bidden to observe? (M. Picktall)

THE ZABUR – THE PSALMS

Sura 17: The Night Journey (Al – Isra): 55b

And we preferred some of the prophets above others, and unto David we gave the psalms.

THE INJIL – THE GOSPEL

Sura 5: The Table (Al – Maida): 46

And we caused Jesus, son of Mary to follow in their footsteps confirming that which was (revealed) before Him, and we bestowed on Him the Gospel wherein is guidance and a light, confirming that which was (revealed) before it in the Torah a guidance and an admonition onto those who ward off (evil).

The Quran bears witness that the Bible was sent down by God Himself.

The Muslims asked Muhammad why is it that the Christians and the Jews did not come to them for judgment and this is the answer that he gave them.

Sura 5: The Table (Al – Maida): 43

How come they unto thee for judgment, when they have the Torah, wherein Allah hath delivered judgment (for them)? Yet even after that they turn away. Such (folk) are not believers.

THE PSALMS

Sura 35: The Originator of Creation (Fatir): 25

And if they deny thee, those before them also denied their messengers. Come unto them with a clear proofs (of Allah's sovereignty) and with the Psalms and the scripture giving light

THE GOSPEL

Sura 5: The Table (Al – Maida): 66a

If they had observed the Torah and the Gospel and that which was revealed unto them from their Lord, they would surely have been nourished from above them and from beneath their feet

The Old and the New Testament agreed with each other.

Sura 5: The Table (Al – Maida): 44a; 46

Lo! We did reveal the Torah. Where is guidance and light, by which the prophets who surrendered (onto Allah) judge the Jews and the rabbis and the priests (judged) by such of Allah's scripture as they were bidden to observe, and thereunto were they witness.

And We caused Jesus, son of Mary, to follow in their footsteps confirming that which was (revealed) before Him, and We bestowed on Him the Gospel wherein is guidance and a light, Confirming that which was (revealed) before it in the Torah a guidance and an admonition onto those who ward off (evil).

One may ask," You don't accept the Quran why are you quoting from its verses"? We do not need the Quran to prove the authenticity of the Bible, but for the sake of our Muslim friends we have to do so. We are only telling them to accept what their Quran is saying. Since that is their final authority.

GOD'S WORD CANNOT BE CHANGED

It is believed in the Muslim sector that the Bible that we are having now is not the Bible that was in existence at the time of Muhammad. But let us again see what the Quran says about this.

Sura 6: Cattle (Al – An'am) 34b

34b. there is none to alter the decisions of Allah. Already there hath reached thee (somewhat) of the tidings of the messengers (We sent before).

The Quran also contains passages from the Bible. If it is corrupt, then the Quran too is corrupt and wrong for to have anything to do with the Bible.

Sura 5: The Table (Al – Maida): 45 & Exodus 2: 23 – 25.

And we prescribed for them therein the life for the life, and the eye for the eye, and the nose for the nose, and the ear for the ear, and the tooth for the tooth, and for relation. But who so forgeoth it (in the way of charity) it shall be expiation for him. Who so judgeth not by that which Allah hath revealed: Such are the wrongdoers.

Exodus 21: 23-25

23 And if any mischief follows, then thou shalt give life for life,
24 Eye for eye, tooth for tooth, hand for hand, foot for foot,
25 Burning for burning wound for wound, stripe for stripe.

Sura 7: The Heights (Al-A'raf): 40

Lo! They who deny our revelations and scorn them, for them the gates of Heaven will not be open nor will they enter the garden until the camel goeth through the needle's eye. Thus do we request the guilty?

Matthew 19:24

And again I say unto you, it is easier for a camel to go through the eye of a needle, than for a rich man to enter into the kingdom of God.

Beside these the Quran has a lot of narrations from the Bible. This is just to mention a few for the sake of time and space.

In the Quran the Jews are sometimes accused of concealing the "the truth" knowingly and twisting their tongues.

In giving answers to questions asked them, and casting (tattooing) the word behind their backs.

It can be noticed that these accusations are against the Jews, but not the Bible and the Christians.

Some Muslim writers speak of many different readings to be found in the Bible, and say that proves the corruption of its text. But this is baseless.

The text of the Bible has never been rectified or dieted by 'UTMHMAN' as was the Quran.

Nor have we had a 'MARWAN' to burn the most ancient copy spread even by the 'UTHMAN'. The word of our God shall stand forever.

Sura 10: Jonah 94a

And if thou (Muhammed) art in doubt concerning that which we reveal unto thee, then question those who read the scripture (that was) before thee.

This was the advice given to Muhammad by Allah. So what can we say about the scriptures in his time? Be the judge for yourself.

Chapter Three

CONTRADICTIONS IN THE BIBLE

---------------------------------- ❂ ----------------------------------

If a book were not a word from God in the first place, no amount of faithful transmission would ever make it the word of God.

Conversely, if a book in its original form were indeed the word of God, variant readings and copyist error would not negate the divine Authority of its ascertainable teachings, especially when the errors and the readings can be identified and when they do not alter the general message of the book as a whole.

1. FIFTY THOUSAND ERRORS

Deedat, a Muslim scholar, reproduced a page from a magazine entitled 'AWAKE' dating some forty-four years ago (published by the JEHOVAH'S WITNESSES, a Christian cult). Claiming that there are some 'Modern Students' who say that "there are 'probably fifty million errors in the Bible".

Very significantly no mention is made of the identity of these so-called modern students, nor is any evidence given of this alleged errors. Of these fifty million, he produced just four for our consideration. Let us look at them.

The first and presumably foremost 'error' is found in Isaiah 7:14

Therefore the Lord himself shall give you a sign; Behold, <u>a virgin</u> shall conceive, and bear a son, and shall call his name Immanuel. (KJV)

Therefore the Lord himself will give you a sign: <u>a young woman</u> will be with child and will give birth to a son, and will call him Immanuel. (RSV)

According to Deedat, this is supposed to be one of the foremost defects in the Bible.

The word 'virgin' in the original Hebrew is 'almah', a word found in every Hebrew text of Isaiah.

So nothing has been done about the original text. The main issue here is purely one of interpretation and translation.

The common Hebrew word for virgin is 'Bethulah' whereas 'Almah' often refers to a young woman and always an unmarried one.

So the RSV translation is a perfectly good literal rendering of the word. The most important point is that the translator must make sure the real meaning or the real message is carried out.

Almost all the English translators used the word 'virgin'. The only simple reason being that the context of the word demands such an interpretation.

Muslims who translated the Quran into English have the same problem with the original Arabic text.

A literal rendering of a word or a text may lose the implied meaning in the original language.

Isaiah used 'Almah' rather than 'Bethulah' because the latter word does not only mean a virgin but also a chaste widow as in Joel 1:8

Joel 1:8

Mourn like a virgin in sackcloth grieving for the husband of her youth;

So that of the RSV gives us the literal meaning and that of the KJV, NIV etc. give us the meaning in context.

A very important question to note is that 'is the young woman a virgin?' If so then we have no problem here.

It has absolutely nothing to do with the textual integrity of the Bible and as such cannot be said to be an error.

2. 'BEGOTTEN SON' AND 'ONLY SON'

John 3:16 (KJV AND NIV)

For God so loved the world, that he gave his <u>only begotten</u> Son, that whosoever believeth in him should not perish, but have everlasting life. (KJV)

"For God so loved the world that he gave his one and <u>only Son</u>, that whoever believes in him shall not perish but have eternal life. (NIV)

The KJV says "the only begotten" and the NIV like the RSV says "his only son". This led Deedat to say that the Bible has been changed because of the omission "begotten"

Once again like the first one, the original Greek word has not been changed; it is just a matter of interpretation and translation. And these two make the same point. Jesus is the unique "son of God".

In the same way, to illustrate our point further, we can refer to Deedat's quote from Sura 19:88

Christians say that God most Gracious has begotten a son (Yusuf Ali)

Christians say that the Beneficent hath taken unto Himself a son (Pickhall, Muhammad Ali and Maulang Daryodadi)

Here we have "begotten" and "taken". I would be happy if my Muslim friends would know and appreciate what is called translation and interpretation. We see the same thing in the Qur'anic interpretation into English.

3. DAVID NUMBERS THE FIGHTING MEN

2 Samuel 24:1

Again the anger of the LORD burned against Israel, and he incited David against them, saying, "Go and take a census of Israel and Judah."

1 Chronicles 21:1

Satan rose up against Israel and incited David to take a census of Israel

Anyone with a reasonable knowledge of scriptures and the Quran will immediately perceive that what is in view here is an inadequate understanding of a feature of the Theology of books.

In the Quran we read: Sura 19 Mary (Mariam): 83

Seest thou that we have set the devils on the disbelievers to confound them with confusion?

Here we just read that Allah sets devil on unbelievers. Though it was Allah who sets them to confusion, but He uses the devil to do so.

In the same way, the same thing happened in the life of David and Israel. Similarly the same things happened to Job, too.

Satan was given power over Job (Ayub in the Quran) to afflict him but later God spoke as if it were He who was moved against him.

Whenever Satan provokes men, the action also can be described indirectly as the movement of God, since without His permission, Satan could not do or achieve anything.

This quote from Zamakhshari's commentary on Sura 2 The Cow (Al-Baqara):7, expresses this point:

Allah hath sealed their hearing and their hearts and their eyes there is a covering. Theirs will be an awful doom.

It is not, in reality, Satan or the unbeliever who seals his heart. Since it was God who granted to him the ability to seal, the sealing was ascribed to him in the same sense as an act, which he has caused.

4.   ASCENSION OF JESUS

The fourth point contains an interesting fallacy. Deedat said the 'inspired' authors of the canonical gospel did not record a single word about the "ascension of Jesus".

This thing is worth looking at The Ascension of Jesus in the gospel of Mark and Luke, which the RSV has identified as being among the variant readings apart from these verses, the gospel writers allegedly make no reference of any nature whatsoever to the ascension. But on the contrary, all the four gospel writers talked about it.

John 20:17

Jesus said, "Do not hold on to me, for I have not yet returned to the Father. Go instead to my brothers and tell them, 'I am returning to my Father and your Father, to my God and your God."

Luke not only wrote his gospel but also, he mentioned it in Acts

Acts 1:9

"After he said this, he was taken up before their very eyes, and a cloud hid him from their sight."

Matthew and Mark also speak about the second coming of Jesus from heaven.

Matthew 26:64

"Yes, it is as you say," Jesus replied. "But I say to all of you: In the future you will see the Son of Man sitting at the right hand of the Mighty One and coming on the clouds of heaven."

Mark 14:62

"I am," said Jesus. "And you will see the Son of Man sitting at the right hand of the Mighty One and coming on the clouds of heaven." (NIV)

It is very difficult to see how Jesus could come from heaven if He has not ascended.

In conclusion we must point out that the passages Mark 16: 9-20 and John 8: 1-11 have not been removed from the Bible and later restored, as Deedat has suggested.

This text has now been included in the RSV translation because scholars are persuaded they are indeed part of the original text.

The truth of the matter is that in our oldest scripts these are found in some text and not in others. So the RSV is merely trying to bring our English translation as close as possible to the original text.

To end it all, this does not tell us that all the original manuscripts, those on which the books of the Bible were written for the first time, are now lost and perished.

For the same truth of the Quran, the oldest text of the Quran still existed dates from the second century after the Hijrah and was written on vellum in the early Al-mail Arabic script. All the other old text of the Quran is in Kufic script and date from the late second century (after the Hijrah) as well.

Chapter Four

IS THE QURAN THE WORD OF GOD?

Our Muslim brethren assert that the eloquence and the beauty of the style of the Quran are a miracle, and thus, the Quran itself is a sufficient proof of Muhammad's Prophetic Office and Divine Commission.

In proof of this peerlessness of the Quran, they quote the challenge to produce verses like: -

Sura 17: The Night Journey (Al – Isra) 89

And verily we have displayed for mankind in this Quran all kinds of similitude, but most of mankind refused aught save disbelief.

This is not convincing enough, because there has been a similar unlettered writer like the RIG-VEDA in India composed between 1000 BC and 1500 BC, long before any written characters were known in India. This was not composed by one man and is so much greater in volume than the Quran.

The opinion that this was so, rests entirely upon the term 'An-nabiyal ummi' in:-

Sura 7: The Heights (Al-A'raf) 158

Say (O Muhammad): O mankind! Lo! I am the messenger of Allah to you all – (the messenger of) Him unto whom belongeth the sovereignty of the heavens and the earth.

There is no God save Allah, He quickeneth and He giveth death so believe in Allah and His messenger, the messenger who <u>cannot read nor write</u>. Who believed in Allah and his words and follow him that haply ye may be led a right.

This does not mean the "the unlettered Prophet" but "the Gentile Prophet". This is clear from:

Sura 3: The Imrans (Al- Imran): 20

And if they argue with thee, (O Muhammad) say: I have surrendered my purpose to Allah and so have those who follow me. And say unto those who have received the scripture and those who read out not: Have ye too surrendered and if they surrender, then truly they are rightly guided and if they turn away, then it is their duty only to convey the message, Allah is seer of His bond man.

The Qufic alphabet was first used to write the Quran destitute of diacritical point and vowel signs. Later they noticed the imperfection of the alphabets.

Whether the Qufic alphabet was that which the Quran is supposed to have been written on the "preserved tablets" in heaven, the writer of the pages does not know.

When any verse was dictated by Muhammad and written down, a pious Muslim soon learnt it by heart by. But occasionally, before this is done, some of the verses would have been lost already, if we may pay attention to tradition (the hadiths).

For instance, in the Mishkatul Masabih, the traditional Muslim informs us that Ayisha (wife of Muhammad) said, "Among what was sent down of the Quran were ten well-known verses about sucking, which were annulled by five well-known ones". (Then the apostle deceased, and they were in that which was recited of the Quran.

So those who do not know would still recite it but it is not part of the Quran today.

Another example is a verse on stoning, instead of this we have in Sura 24 Light (Al-Nur): 1-5. - The penalty of hundred stripes for crime.

Sura 24 Light (Al-Nur): 1-5.

Ayisha said, "The verse on stoning and sucking came. And its sheets were under my bed, when therefore the apostle of God died and were occupied about his death a tame animal (goat) came in and ate it".

Muslims quote Abu Musa Al Ashari as saying to five hundred recites of the Quran at Basrah, "Verily we used to recite a Sura which is in length (long verses) and severity, we used to compare to Baraah another name for Suratu Taubah. i.e. Sura 10 and I have forgotten.

It is well known that Ubai added to his copy of the Quran short Suras entitled respectively Suratul Khala and Suratul Hafd. (This is known later as Suratul Qanut) Because he affirms that they were part of the original Quran but had been removed or omitted by 'UTMAN'.

On the other hand, Ibn Musud omitted Surahs 1,113 and114.

Some of the Shia party said that certain words relating to Ali have been purposely omitted from the present text of the Quran in *Sura: - 4: 136,164; 5:71; 26:228.*

They said that in Sura 3:104, the word Ummatin "nations" has been put there for the original word 'aimmatin' – Imams.

Moreover, it is declared that, the whole Sura, called the Suratun Nurain, has been purposely omitted from the Quran. This Sura was quoted by full length (long verses) by Mirza Muhsin of Kashmir surnamed Al fani, in his Dabistani Mazahib.

HOW THE QURAN WAS BROUGHT TOGETHER

We have now inquired the way the scattered Sura were brought together. Al Bukhari informs us that, apparently about a year after Muhammad's death, Zaid IbnThabit first put the Quran together at the command of Khalifah Abu Bakr but at the end of the collection, Zaid said a lot of the Suras and the verse has been lost during the slaughter at Al-Yamamah, which also includes the reciters.

It is said that 700 fell, Uthman later sent to every region that the Quran should be burned, because Zaid has now realized that "suratul Ahzab" has been omitted.

From this, it is evident that some differences existed between the revised copies of the Quran issued by Uthman and the original "sheets" which Hafsah had, in her keeping.

WHY THE QURAN IS IN ARABIC

Learned men are now aware that the dialect of the Quraish is the old language of Mecca, not that of the paradise.

Arabic is one of the Semitic tongues. Its sisters are Hebrew, Aramic, Ethiopic, Syriac, Assyrian and other tongues of less importance.

Yet at the same time scholars rightly inform us that the words of the Quran are not one language, but mixed up, especially names and places.

Know, therefore, that the Quran descended in the language of the Arabs and in accordance with their style of eloquence and all of them understood it and knew its various meanings in several parts and in their relation to one another.

Sura 14: (Ibrahim): 4

And we never sent a messenger, save with the language of his folks, that he might make (the message) clear for them. Then Allah sendeth whom He will astray, and guideth whom He will. He is the mighty, the wise.

Chapter Five

CONTRADICTIONS IN THE QURAN

"A proof of the inspiration of the Quran is that, it is wonderful and free from self-contradiction. Some Muslims say that in so large a book there must have occurred many contradictory statements, if it were not divinely originated.

Simply put, contradiction means to declare the opposite of (a statement) to be true; be at variance with."

Let us see if what we have just read is true. We are just going to compare a few verses and chapters.

Sura 16: (Al-Wahl): 101

And when we put a revelation in a place of (another) revelation and Allah knoweth best what He revealeth- they say: Lo! Thou art but inventing, most of them know not.

Sura 2: (Al-Baqara): 106

Such of our revelations as we abrogate (change) or cause to be forgotten, we bring (in place) one better or the like there of. Knowest thou not that Allah is able to do all things?

Actually these two verses bring the whole trouble. It just means that Allah can say something now and later think that He should have said it another way instead of that way.

So He would later change what He said. These things are there because of the way the Quran was compiled. Just let us take a few verses and compare them.

1.   Sura 56: (Al-Waqi'a): 11- 14

Those are they who will be brought nigh. In gardens of delight; A multitude of old and <u>a few of those of later time.</u>

Sura 56 (Al-Waqi'a): 38-40

For those on the right hand; a multitude of those of old, and <u>a multitude of those of later time</u>.

And a few of those of later time and a multitude of those of later time.

The second scripture put the first scripture in a serious confusion; the first reads a few of those of later time.

The second scripture reads a multitude of those of later time. So which is one is the correct verse?

2.   Sura 4: (Al- Nisa): 116

Lo! Allah pardoneth not that partners should be ascribed unto Him. He pardoneth all save to whom He will. Whoso ascribed partners unto Allah hath wondered far astray.

Sura 2: (Al-Baqara): 34

And when we said unto the angels: Fall down prostrate before Adam and they fell prostrate save Iblis (Lucifer), he said: shall I fall prostrate before that which thou hast created of clay?

Although it is an unpardonable sin to worship any other but Allah, the Quran teaches that Satan (Azaric or Iblis) was cast down from heaven because he refused to worship Adam.

3.   Sura 47: (Muhammad): 15

A similitude of the Garden which those who keep their duty (to Allah) are promised: Therein are rivers of water unpolluted, and rivers of milk whereof the flavor changeth not, and rivers of wine delicious to the drinkers, and rivers of clear run honey; therein for them is every kind of fruit, with pardon from their Lord. (Are those who enjoy all this) like those who are immortal in the Fire and are given boiling water to drink so that it teareth their bowels?

Drink is not allowed in Islam but they are promise a lot of wine in paradise.

Chapter Six

CONTRADICTIONS BETWEEN THE QURAN AND THE BIBLE

---- ✸ ----

If the Quran actually came to confirm and protect the Taurat and the Injil, which had been revealed before it, then there should be total agreement between these writings.

They should not have to contradict each other. They have to be in total harmony and should not differ in simple things like names, events, the deity of Christ, and many others.

All the same let us try and find out for ourselves. Let us pick a few examples to elaborate the point.

Sura 3: The Imrans (Al – Imrans): 3

He has revealed unto thee (Muhammad) the scripture with truth, confirming that which was (revealed) before it, even as He revealed the Torah and the Gospel.

Point A

1. Sura 6: Cattle (Al – An'am): 74 & Genesis 11:26

74 (Remember) when Abraham said unto his father Azar: takest thou Idols for gods? I see thee and thy folk in error manifest.

23

Genesis 11: 26

26 Now Terah lived seventy years, and begot Abram, Nahor, and Haran

The name of Abraham's father was Terah and not Azar.

Point B

2. Sura 28: The Narrative (Al – Qasas): 9 & Exodus 2:5–9

And the wife of Pharaoh said: (He will be) a consolation for me and for thee. Kill Him not. Peradventure he may be of use to us, or we may choose him for a son. And they perceived not.

Exodus 2:5

5 Then the daughter of Pharaoh came down to bathe at the river. And her maidens walked along the riverside; and when she saw the ark among the reeds, she sent her maid to get it.

Instead of Pharaohs daughter-adopting Moses the Quran refers to her as Pharaoh's wife.

Point C

1. Sura 19: Mary (Mariam): 27-28

Then she brought him to her own folk, carrying him. They said; O Mary! Thou hast come with an amazing thing. Oh! Sister of Aaron! Thy father was not a wicked man nor was thy mother a harlot.

2. Exodus 15:20

And Miriam the prophetess, the sister of Aaron, took a timbrel in her hand: and all the women went out after her with timbrels and with dances.

Miriam the sister of Aaron was here mistaken for Mary the mother of Jesus.

There are lots of comparisons that we can do, but we would discuss some more later because most of the Bible narrations quoted in the Quran are different from what is in the Bible.

Chapter Seven

MUHAMMAD IN THE QURAN

He was asserted to be the bearer of a unique message from God. A revelation greater than any that had been reached and that the Quran, which he recited, had been dictated to him by Angel Gabriel.

To prove his claim, it was necessary for him to prove his ministry by the working of miracles, like what happened in the Bible. The question then is did he perform any miracle at all?'

First and foremost, who is a Prophet? Simply put, he is someone upon whom the Spirit of God rests, to foretell God's purpose for the past, present and the future; someone who can speak the mind of God and understands the times and the seasons of God and has foreknowledge concerning the future.

John the Baptist was called a prophet, not because he performed any miracle but he was able to speak the mind of God concerning the future.

The Quran did not say anything like that about Muhammad. Indeed, since the Quran is the final Authority of Islam, it must be the definite book that contains something about that and not any other book, not even the Haditts. So let us find out;

1. *Sura 6: Cattle (Al-An'am) 37*

They say: why hath no potent been sent down upon him from his Lord? Say; Lo! Allah is able to send down potent. But most of them know not.

He knew that there was nothing he could do, so Allah asked him to wait with those who wanted to see a miracle.

There have been lots of such incidents in the Bible where people have put demands on the prophets, e.g. in the case of Elijah and the Baal prophets.

He said Allah was able to send down a miracle, but Allah never did for him (Muhammad).

2. *Sura 6: Cattle (Al-An'am) 50*

Say (O Muhammad to the disbelievers): I say not unto you that I possess the treasures of Allah nor that I have Knowledge of the unseen; and I say not unto you: Lo! I am an angel. I follow only that which is inspired in me. Are the blind man and the seer equal? Will ye not then take thought?

This is a serious statement by him because a Prophet is supposed to be a mouthpiece for God. He must have knowledge of the unseen. He must understand the times and the seasons. But Muhammad has no idea what goes on in the realm of the supernatural.

3. *Sura 6: Cattle (Al-An'am) 109*

And they swear a solemn oath by Allah that if there come unto them a portent they would

Believe therein. Say portents are with Allah and (so is) that which telleth you that if such came unto them they would not believe.

If they asked him to perform a miracle, he should say only God who can do a miracle. This would clearly suggest that the man had no power to work a miracle.

The 'God' of the Quran commanded Muhammad to say that he is just a mortal messenger any time a miracle was demanded from him.

4.   SURA 29: The Spider (AL-ANKABUT) 50

50. *And they say: why are not o sent down upon him from his Lord? Say: portents are with Allah only, and I am but a plain warner.*

He is just a plain 'warner' and miracles are for Allah only.

There are lots of funny, strange tales told by some Muslims about his miracles.

The question is, did he perform any miracle? If he did, the Quran should be able to answer this puzzle for us, because it is their final authority.

You would hear them say things like:

He called a tree to follow him and it did.

Causing a well water to feed 1,300 to 100,000 and let water to spring from his fingers.

Somebody defected from Islam and Muhammed said the earth would reject the defector's body if he died and it happened so.

Unfortunately, even the Quran has no evidence or record of all these things.

SURA 7: The Heights (AL-A'raf) 188

Say: for myself I have <u>no power to benefit, nor power to hurt</u>, save that which Allah willeth. <u>Had I knowledge of the unseen</u>, I should have abundance of *wealth, and adversity would not touch me. I am but a warner, and a bearer of good tidings unto folk who believe.*

This verse tells us there was nothing spiritual about him; he had no power and also had no knowledge of the unseen and could not even prevent adversity. All these point out that the person in question was not who they claim he is.

Chapter Eight

JESUS IN THE QURAN

---- ✸ ----

It is important for us to find out what the Quran says about Jesus Christ.

We have to know what Muhammad knew about Jesus in his time; not what other people say or what Muslims say and not even what Amed Deedat says. So let us find out what the Quran says.

Sura 3: The Immrans (Al-Imran): 36

And when she was delivered she said: My lord! Lo! I am delivered of a female-Allah knew best of what she was delivered-the male is not as the female; and Lo! I have named her Mary, <u>and lo! I crave thy protection for her and her offspring from Satan the outcast.</u>

Allah chose Mary and prophesied concerning the birth of Jesus Christ.

He knew who Jesus was coming to be, so Allah made Mary a special person and started protecting her before Jesus was even born.

Sura 3: The Imrans (Al-Imran): 45

(And remember) When the angels said: O Mary! Lo! Allah giverth thee glad tidings of <u>a word from Him, Whose name is the Messiah, Jesus, son of Mary,</u> illustrious in the world and the Hereafter, and one of those brought near (unto Allah)

Sura 4: Woman (Al-Nisa): 171

O People of the Scripture! Do not exaggerate in your religion nor utter aught concerning Allah save the truth. The Messiah, Jesus son of Mary, was only a messenger of Allah, <u>and His</u> <u>word</u> which He conveyed unto Mary, and <u>a spirit from Him</u>. So believe in Allah and His messengers, and say not "Three". Cease! (it is) better for you! Allah is only One God. Far is it removed from His transcendent majesty that he should have a son. His is all that is in the heavens and all that is in the earth. And Allah is sufficient as Defender.

There are some key words here I want us to consider. The birth of Jesus was foretold and the angel also told Zakariyya that his son (John) shall confirm the 'Word of Allah' (ruy Allah).

The Quran proves that Jesus is a different 'Person' from all others by making references such as:

He is the Messiah

He is the "Word of God" (Ruy Allah)

He shall be noble in this world and the world to come.

Jesus was born not of a seed of a man.

5. He is the "Spirit of God" (Kalimat Allah)

The Quran teaches that it was God Himself who taught Jesus the scriptures.

We all know and believe that it is only God who can create any life, because He is the giver of life.

Now, the Quran states that Jesus created a bird from the dust (just like how God did in the Bible), created man and also did all manner of miracles, from healing the sick to the raising of the dead.

Sura 3: The Imrans (Al-Imran): 49

And we will make Him a messenger unto the children of Israel, (saying) Lo! I come unto you with a sign from your Lord. Lo! I fashion for you out of clay the likeness of a bird, and I would breathe in to it and it is a bird, by Allah's leave. I heal who was born blind, and the leper, and I raise the dead, by Allah's leave. And I announce unto you what ye eat and what ye store up in your houses. Lo! Herein verily is a portent for you, if ye are to be believers.

He has even been given power to tell Israel what to eat, and to make lawful unto them that, which was forbidden.

The messiah means: The consecrated one (as a king, priest or saint), it also means the anointed. Jesus is the "Word of God" (Ruy- Allah). This confirms what is in the Book of John.

Jesus is also a spirit from God (Kalimatt Allah). He was there before creation. You can see this in the beginning of the book of Genesis.

Sura 66: Prohibition (Al- Tahrim): 12

And Allah has given us example, Imarans daughter, who preserved her chastity and into whose womb <u>we breathed of our Spirit</u>: who put her trust in the words of her lord and His Scriptures and was truly obedient. (Mamud y. Zaid)

In conclusion:

Jesus was there before the world began. The Quran says He is the Breath of The God Almighty, The creator of the universe and "The Word from God". He is the Messiah, the anointed and the consecrated one.

The One Who would sit on the judgment Seat to judge the Nations on that Hour of Doom. He is the mystery of God. In Jesus are hidden all the treasures of wisdom and knowledge.

HOW TO PRESENT THE GOSPEL TO A MUSLIM

He is the image of the invisible God, the firstborn over all creation. For by him all things were created: things in heaven and on earth, visible and invisible, whether thrones or powers or rulers or authorities; all things were created by him and for him.

He is before all things, and in him all things hold together and he is the head of the body, the church; he is the beginning and the firstborn from among the dead, so that in everything he might have the supremacy.

For God was pleased to have all his fullness dwell in him and through him to reconcile to himself all things, whether things on earth or things in heaven, by making peace through his blood, shed on the cross.

References to Him and His name run through The Bible from Genesis to Revelation.

In Genesis	–	Jesus was the Ram at Abraham's altar.
In Exodus	–	He was the Passover Lamb.
In Leviticus	–	He is the High Priest.
In Numbers	–	He was the Cloud by Day and a Pillar of Fire by Night.
In Deuteronomy	–	He was the City of our Refuge.
In Joshua	–	He was the Commander in Chief of the Lords Army.
In Judges	–	He was the Judge.
In Ruth	-	He was our Kings-man Redeemer.
In 1 Samuel and 2 Samuel	–	He was our Trusted Prophet.
In Kings and Chronicles	–	He was our Reigning King.
In Ezra	–	He was the Faithful Scribe.
In Nehemiah	–	He is the Re-Builder of everything that is broken
In Esther	–	He was Mordecai sitting faithfully at the gate.
In Job	–	He is our Redeemer that liveth.
In Psalm	–	He is our Shepherd and we shall not want.

In Proverbs and Ecclesiastes	–	He is our Wisdom.
In Song of Solomon	–	He was the Beautiful Bridegroom.
In Isaiah	–	He was the Suffering servant.
In Jeremiah and Lamentations	–	Jesus was the Weeping Prophet.
In Ezekiel	–	He is the Wonderful Four-Faced Man.
In Daniel	–	He was the Fourth Man in the midst of the fiery furnace.
In Hosea	–	He is our Love that is ever Faithful.
In Joel	–	He baptizes us with the Holy Spirit.
In Amos	–	He was our Burden.
In Obadiah	–	He is our Savior.
Jonah	–	He is the Great Foreign Missionary that who takes the Word of God into the world.
In Micah	–	He is the Messenger with Beautiful Feet.
In Nahum	–	He is the Avenger.
In Habakkuk	–	He is the Watchman that is ever praying for revival.
In Zephaniah	–	He is the Lord Mighty to save.
In Haggai	–	He is the Restorer for our lost heritage.
In Zechariah	–	He is our Fountain.
In Malachi	–	He is the Sun of Righteousness with Healing in His Wings.
In Matthew	–	He is the Christ, The son of the Living God.
In Mark	–	He is the Miracle worker.
In Luke	–	He is the Son of Man.
In John	–	He is the Door by which every one of us must enter.
In Acts	–	He is the Shining light that appears to Saul, on the road to Damascus.
In Romans	-	He is our Justifier.
In 1 & 2 Corinthians	–	He is our Resurrection.
In Galatians	–	He redeems us from the law.
In Ephesians	–	He is our unsearchable Riches.

HOW TO PRESENT THE GOSPEL TO A MUSLIM

In Philippians	–	He supplies our every need.
In Colossians	–	The Fullness of the Godhead Bodily dwells in Him.
In 1 & 2 Thessalonians	–	He is our soon-coming King.
In 1 & 2 Timothy	–	He is the Mediator between God and Man.
In Titus	–	He is our Blessed Hope.
In Philemon	–	He is the Friend that sticks closer than a Brother.
And in Hebrews	–	He is the Blood of the Everlasting Covenant.
In James	–	He is the Lord that heals the sick.
In 1 & 2 Peter	–	He is the Chief shepherd.
In 1, 2 & 3 John	–	He has the Tenderness of love.
In Jude	–	He is the Lord coming with the Ten Thousand saints.
And In Revelation	–	He is the King of Kings and the Lord of Lords.

Chapter Nine

CALL OF MUHAMMAD INTO MINISTRY

---------------------- ✸ ----------------------

It is said that he was raised as an apostle. The call came when he was 40 years old and when he was with Khadijah in a cave in mount Hira near Mecca.

He thought that Angel Gabriel came to him to let him recite in the name of the Lord (Allah). Actually it was Khadijah who encouraged him to accept the challenge.

Was he able to stand the challenge? He had no word of knowledge or word of wisdom. Every prophet should know the future and be able to perform miracles like other prophets in the Bible.

God Jehovah used every one of them to predict the future or perform miracles. They sometimes knew and understood the times and the seasons and knew what Israel had to do.

If truly Mohammad was the seal of the prophets, these should be nothing even if he was challenged to perform a miracle, same was done to Moses and Elijah and that proved their ministry.

He had this to say about himself:

SURA 46: (Al-Ahqaf) 9

9: say: I am no new <u>thing</u> among the messengers (of Allah) nor know I what will be done with me or with you. I do but follow that which is inspired in me, and I am but a plain warner.

From this verse, Muhammad described himself as a "thing" and the 'thing' is normally used to describe lifeless entities. This really tells us how Muhammad saw himself and that he was no one special.

Ayishah tells us that, when Mohammad was asked how inspiration came to him, he said: "Sometimes they came to me as it were the ringing of a bell, and it is very violent upon me.

It leaves me, and I recollect what it said. And sometimes the angel appears to me like a man and converses with me and I remember what he says"

On the authority of 'Amr ibn sharhabel, it is stated that Muhammad said to Khadijah, "when I was alone I heard a cry. O' Mohammad, O' Mohammad"

In tradition it is stated that he said, "I fear lest I should become a magician least one should say I am a follower of the Jinn," and again, "I fear lest there should be madness or demoniac possession in me."

After an accession of shivering and shutting his eyes, there used to come over him what resembled a swoon, his face would foam, and he would roar like a young camel. U'mar ibnul Khattab says, "When inspiration descended on the Apostles of Allah, there used to be heard near his face as it were the buzzing of bees."

This strange phenomenon did not begin in Mohammad's case. Just before he claimed to be a prophet from his childhood we know only a few facts, one of them is, when he was quite a young boy, living in the desert with his foster-parents, something similar occurred.

This is from Anas in Mishkat, "As for the Apostle of Allah, Gabriel came to him while he was playing with the (other) lads. He took him and threw him on the ground and split his heart then he took out of it a drop of clotted blood and said: this is Satan's portion of thee.

Then he washed it (the heart) in a basin of Gold, in Zamzam-water. Then he repaired it and restored it to its place. And the child run home and said: "Verily Mohammad has been killed".

Anas said, "I used to see the mark of the needle on his chest."

This question then arises: How can it be proved that the phenomenon which traditions mention denoted the visits of Gabriel to bring inspiration upon him?

Some of our Muslim readers have doubtlessly studied the science of medicine. Others have abled physicians among their friends. Let them, therefore, inquire whether there is a disease, often beginning in early youth or childhood, among the symptoms of which are some of the following.

The patient utters a strange, inarticulate cry, falls suddenly to the ground and becomes pale then sometimes turns purple, the body trembles violently, the mouth foams, the eyes are shut and at the point of death, sees beams of light and bright colours, hears a ringing in his ears and frequently suffers after the attack from a most violent headache. He often has a distinct warning before a fit comes on.

It has been asserted that there is such a disease, and that is not very rare. The author of these pages is not a physician, for which cause, among others, he does not venture to give any opinion on the subject.

We will, therefore, leave it to our readers to consider and by God's guidance, to decide. Let it never be forgotten that the statements about him, which we have quoted, are not from his enemies but loved ones who believed and still believe that he is the seal of the prophets and an Apostle of God.

Chapter Ten

DOES THE BIBLE CONTAIN PROPHECIES ABOUT MUHAMMAD?

❋

If God had intended to send into the world a prophet far greater than Jesus Christ was, then we should naturally expect to find predictions concerning that prophet in the Old Testament and more so in the New Testament.

It is believed, mostly by Muslims that, it used to be in the Bible that Mohammad was the seal of all the prophets but Jews and Christians have now removed it from the Bible.
We need not to talk about this because we have talked about it already in the authenticity of the Bible (Refer to Chapter 2).

The Bible is much older than Mohammad and the Quran. So the question is, was the reference to Mohammed removed before or after the birth of Mohammad, because he never told us in the Quran that the Bible had been changed or altered.

It would be very appropriate to consider the written dates of some of the Biblical manuscripts. The last book of the Old Testament was compiled in 400 BC. Even from the event of Noah's flood in 2000 BC till Malachi (400 BC), nothing was said about Mohammad.

Then, for the New Testament: the Book of Acts was written by Dr. Luke in Rome (about AD 60); Galatians by Paul in Ephesus (about AD 57);

2 Timothy by Paul in Rome (about AD 67); 1 Corinthians by Paul in Macedonia (about AD 55); Romans by Paul in Corinth (about AD 58); the Ephesians by Paul in Rome (about AD 61) and the Gospel of Luke by Dr. Luke in Caesura (about AD 59).

Almost all the manuscripts of the Bible had been written before the dispersion of the Jews in AD 70. Only the last book, Revelations, was written in about AD 100 in which the writer did not have any bias against the Prophet of Islam who was born in AD 570.

So the book had been in existence for about 500 years before Mohammed was born in AD 570. If the text of the Bible, as we now have it contains genuine predictions of Muhammad's coming, we Christians must accept it in good faith but unfortunately this is not so.

We now proceed first to examine the chief passages of the Old Testament in which our Muslim brethren claim to find predictions regarding Mohammad.

THE OLD TESTAMENT

1. GENESIS 49:8, 10

8 Judah, thou art he whom thy brethren shall praise: thy hand shall be in the neck of thine enemies; and thy father's children shall bow down before thee.

10. The scepter shall not depart from Judah, nor a lawgiver from between his feet, until Shiloh come and unto him shall the gathering of the people be. (KJV)

This is asserted by Muslims to refer to Mohammad, especially because 'Judah' in verse 8 means "Praise" as does the name Mohammad.

Note also that the passage is a prophetic statement by Jacob to his son Judah concerning him and his future descendants. Jacob at the time was pronouncing blessings or prophetic directions for each of his sons. Also, the context shows that Shiloh was to be born among the descendants of Judah and Shiloh is a direct reference to Jesus Christ. Indeed,

Shiloh is one of the names of Jesus Christ

Mohammad was of the Arabian Tribe of the Quraish. He was not a Jew. The Arabic verb 'Hamada' is not like the Jewish verb 'to praise'.

Shiloh is a title of the Messiah (Jesus Christ) and the Samaritan Targum implies this also. Jesus was born of the tribe of Judah, and the Gentiles have already in large measure, become obedient unto him.

When an argument is raised by Muslims that the promised prophet that Moses talk of was not to rise among the Israelites ("from the midst of thee" does not occur in the Septuagint or the Samaritan Pentateuch, "For Moses truly said unto the fathers, A prophet shall the Lord your God raise up unto you of your brethren, like unto me; him shall ye hear in all things whatsoever he shall say unto you.")

When you read through the book of Genesis chapter twenty five, you will appreciate that it gave the genealogy of Ishmael and that he died in the midst of his own descendants.

Ishmael was a brother to Isaac and not Judah. The many uses of the word 'brethren' by Moses to the Israelites was always understood to refer to themselves as children of one man, Israel also called Jacob.

They also state that no such prophet did rise among the Israelites, referring to:

If one continues to read up to verse twelve of Deuteronomy chapter thirty four, it is clear that the statement referred to no other prophet being used in exactly the same way as Moses was. I challenge anyone to name even one other prophet like Moses.

The only one who was put on a similar platform with Moses as to what they brought into the world is our Lord and Savior Jesus Christ.

Is it true that Mohammed was like Moses in many ways as Muslims claim? For example, that both were brought up in their enemies' houses; that both appeared among idolaters; that both were at first rejected by their own people and afterwards accepted by them; that each gave a law; that each fled from their enemies (Moses to Midian and Mohammed to Medinah, a name of a similar meaning); that each marched to battle against their enemies and enabled their followers to conquer Palestine.

In reply to this, Deuteronomy chapter thirty four verse ten refers only to the time at which it was written, and the word "since" may be said to imply the expectation that such a prophet would arise "in Israel", not outside. The words "from the midst of thee" are almost certainly genuine, though even without them the meaning is clear. Mohammad did not arise in Israel.

Moreover, the Taurat (books of the law written by Moses) clearly says that no prophet was to be expected from Ishmael, for God's covenant was made with Isaac, not with Ishmael.

The Quran also, in several places, speaks of the prophetic office as having been entrusted to Isaac's seed.

Sura 29: The spider (Al-Ankabut) 27

And we bestowed on him Isaac and Jacob, and we have established the Prophethood and the scripture among his seed and we gave him reward in the world and lo! In the hereafter he verily is among the righteous.

The promised Prophet was to be sent to Israel: But Mohammad professed to be sent to the Arabs among whom he was born.

The two ways in which the Israelites expected the coming prophet to resemble Moses were: (1) Personal knowledge of God, and (2) Mighty works

It is in the traditions that Mohammad said, "we have not known thee in truth of thy knowledge (as thou should be known)" with reference to the mighty works, the Quran tells us that Mohammad has not been given the power to do miracles.

However, the Quran bears witness that Moses did a lot of miracles.

God has made things clear in the Bible to show that, that prophecy refers to Christ and not Mohammad. Jesus explains that he is the one that Moses talks about. For Bible says that, for had ye believed Moses, ye would have believed me; for he wrote of me.

Psalm 45:2-6, 13

2. Thou art fairer than the children of men: grace is poured into thy lips: therefore God hath blessed thee forever.

3. Gird thy sword upon thy thigh, O most mighty, with thy glory and thy majesty.

4. And in thy majesty ride prosperously because of truth and meekness and righteousness; and thy right hand shall teach thee terrible things.

5. Thine arrows are sharp in the heart of the king's enemies; whereby the people fall under thee.

6. Thy throne, O God, is forever and ever: the sceptre of thy kingdom is a right sceptre.

13. The king's daughter is all glorious within: her clothing is of wrought gold.

This is said to be a prophecy regarding Mohammad, since he is called "The Prophet with the sword" and it is thought that verses 3-5 are especially applicable to him, but there are two answers to refute this theory.

This is just to talk about a few things in the Old Testament and hopefully you are convinced that the so-called references to Mohammad are baseless. Let us look at a few more things from the New Testament.

THE NEW TESTAMENT

A.

John 1:21

They asked him, "Then who are you? Are you Elijah?" He said, "I am not." "Are you the Prophet?" He answered, "No."

Some Muslims take the words "Elias (Elijah) indeed cometh" as a prediction of Muhammad's advent, but Christ said in His time that Elias 'is come already and they knew him not' i.e. they did not recognize him and ended up killing him instead.

Of course John the Baptist was not Elijah in person, for transmigration was not taught in the Bible; therefore, he answered no.

He was asked whether he was the Christ's forerunner, appointed before birth to go before Him "in the Spirit and power of Elijah" as the angel had predicted and in this sense, as Malachi had foretold. He came as Elijah living in much the same way as the latter had done, often in the desert.

These had nothing to do with Muhammad neither by lifestyle, ministry nor calling even if any.

B.   Mark 1:7

7. And this was his message: "After me will come one more powerful than I, the thongs of whose sandals I am not worthy to stoop down and untie.

Muslims often say that "The Injil contains the words of Jesus" and so according to them, in Mark 1:7, Jesus prophesied of Muhammad saying "there cometh after me he that is mightier than I". Funny they say that, since nothing is further from the truth. In the said passage, it is clear that this was John the Baptist speaking and he was speaking of no other person than Jesus.

The Jews mention three prophets in succession, Christ, Elijah and the Prophet; and that should be Muhammad and that John did not contradict them. The prophet, they assert, was Muhammad who was foretold in the book of Deuteronomy (I will raise up for them a prophet like you from among their brothers; I will put my words in his mouth, and he will tell them everything I command him.) It cannot be Christ or Elijah who were mentioned separately.

Let it be noted that Jesus did mention that John the Baptist was a prophet although John himself always refused to take accolades for himself, showing his humility.

C. John 14:30

I will not speak with you much longer, for the prince of this world is coming. He has no hold on me.

"The Prince of the world cometh". Many Muslims consider that these words of Christ are a prediction of the coming of Muhammed but in the first place, the context shows that here Christ was not speaking of a prophet, who was to come after Him, for He adds, "and he hath nothing in me". This means the person spoken of was the enemy of all that is good, which cannot be said to refer to any prophet. Indeed, Jesus was here referring to Satan, the devil.

In conclusion all the manuscripts of the Bible had been written before the dispersion of the Jews in AD 70. Only Revelations was written in about AD 100 in which the writer did not have any bias against the Prophet of Islam who was born in AD 570. So the book had been in existence for about 500 years before Mohammed was born and 40 years before the birth of Islam. If the text of the Bible, as we now have it, contains genuine predictions of Muhammad's coming, Christians must accept it in good faith but unfortunately, this is not so.

Printed in the United States
By Bookmasters